On Their Own

Adventure Athletes in Solo Sports

By Steve Boga

BOOK TWO

HNB

HIGH NOON BOOKS
Novato, California

International Standard Book Number: 0-87879-926-5

0 9 8 7 6 5
0 9 8 7 6 5 4 3

Library of Congress Cataloging-in-Publication Data

Boga, Steve. 1947—
    On their own: adventure athletes in solo sports/by Steve Boga.
        p.   cm.
    Summary: Describes the training, determination, and personal triumphs of such athletes as motorcycle racer Kenny Roberts, long distance runner Ann Trason, and speed skater Eric Heiden.
    ISBN 0-87879-928-1
    1. Athletes—United States—Biography.   2. Determination (Personality trait)   [1. Athletes.]   I. Title.
GV697.A1B555   1992
796'.0922—dc20
[B]   92-15762
                                                               CIP
                                                                AC

Contents

Ann Trason Concentrates on the Race

Ann Trason
Trail Runner

See Ann run and run and run. See the big smile on her face. She loves to run. That helps explain her success running long distances faster than any woman alive, faster than 99.9% of the men, too. See Ann's backside as she leaves you in the dust.

See Ann Trason resting at an aid station in the middle of a 100-mile race. You probably will not be too impressed. She looks more like a skinny teenager than a world-class runner. Ann is dressed in a T-shirt, scarf, dirty shoes, and a hat pulled down low. She looks like a kid on a paper route.

———————————

Later, in a busy Berkeley cafe having dinner, she looks pretty. She wears earrings and a little makeup. Her shoulder length brown hair is no longer pressed against her forehead. Her clothes, blue jeans, blouse and sandals, seem to fit well. They also are not stained with sweat.

Ann has high cheekbones and thin lips. She seems shy but has a friendly smile. She looks younger than her 29 years. When asked why she runs, she says, "I always did like to move. When I was little, I remember my parents tied bells around my ankles so they could keep track of me."

"By the time I was in the sixth grade, the Presidential Fitness Competition was big. We had to be tested in stupid things like how many sit-ups could we do in 60 seconds and how far we could run in 6 minutes."

Ann's sit-ups did not make the headlines of the school newspaper. But in the six-minute run, she managed to cover nearly a mile. She recalls, "I finished second in the school even though I hated running track."

Her father, a real sports fan, was thrilled by her success. He started dragging Ann out to the track to practice. She says, "Of course, anything your parents want you to do, you don't want to do. I thought running track was boring."

She kept running, but her heart was not in it. A year later, she got sick and could not run track for a year. She found out she missed the sport. "It was something to do after school," she says.

When Ann felt better, she ran longer distances. In high school she often ran 10,000 meters. "That is 24 to 25 times around a track, which is really boring," she says, rolling her eyes.

But she was good at running. In her senior year, Ann came in sixth in the National

Championships. A college in New Mexico gave her a track scholarship. But before she could start school, she hurt her knee. Ann had to give up her plan to go to school at the time. After surgery, she started college at the University of California at Berkeley.

She did not like the track coach at Cal, so she quit the team. Instead she fixed her mind on her studies. She loved science. She ran only once or twice a week. She says, "It was more to release stress than to stay fit. I'd study all evening, then call someone up to go running at midnight."

By the time Ann was done with school, her running career seemed finished. Then a strange thing happened. As an adult, Ann went back to running with more interest than she ever had as a teen. She explains, "Out of school, I took a job doing research at a hospital in San Francisco. It was dull work. Golden Gate Park was right there. So I started running once more. Soon I wanted to run races. So I entered a triathlon (a race with swimming, bicycling and running). I really don't know how athletes train for that race. I would get up to swim at 6:00 a.m. I would run at lunch, then bike at night. I was tired all the time."

This is how Ann talks about her first race. "It was very tough. I lived through it. I crossed the finish line."

Before she could race again, she was hit by a car while bicycling. She had 20 stitches in her arm. Even today she can't straighten that arm. She says, "It hurts when I swim. That is my excuse for not doing one more triathlon."

Instead, she tried a 50-mile race. It was the American 50-Mile Run from Sacramento to Auburn. Even though it was April, it was hot. The temperature at the start was 95 degrees. An hour into the race, a fellow runner moved over to Ann and gave her some friendly advice. He said, "I don't know who you are, but you should have a water bottle." Stubborn but not stupid, she saw her mistake. She borrowed a water bottle.

Ann finished first woman and 13th overall, in 7 hours, 9 minutes. With no teaching or practice, she ran a new course record in her first fifty-mile run. She had to face it. She was a long-distance runner. "I did all right in that race," she says with a modest smile.

Ann felt like setting serious goals for herself for the first time since high school. Her new plan was to run a marathon (26-mile run), an ultra-marathon (a 50- or 100-mile run), the Davis Double (a 200-mile bike ride) and a triathlon (swim, bike, run) all in one year. As it turned out, she finished all but the last race. Ann says, "Problem was, I did the first three in three months, then fell apart. I tried to do a second marathon, but had to drop out. I was ill. I seem to overdo it and then get sick. It is a problem I have learned to deal with."

Some would agree that Ann overdoes it. She runs 120 to 160 miles of roads and trails per week. She must be careful about sleeping and eating, too. Ann must say no even to that first Twinkie. But the hardest is having to say no to friends. She says, "All that time I spend running can cost me friends. I have a list at home of people I should call or do things with." But she knows that most good things come with a price. Her friends will just have to wait.

Why pay such a high price? Why be so serious about a sport? When reporters ask questions like that, she curls her upper lip. "I am not that serious. It's fun. That's why I do it. When it is not fun anymore, I will quit."

She likes what former world-class track star, Lee Evans, once said. "I love to run just to feel the wind in my hair."

"It is the same way for me," she says with a bright smile.

11

Ann often runs alone. But she likes people. Most of all, she likes the down-to-earth folks who do long trail runs. She says, "They enjoy the outdoors, and they are not all in love with their fancy cars."

Only about one runner out of every eight is a woman. Ann would like to see that change. "A lot of women are still too busy taking care of their boyfriends," she says sadly.

"Some men who run can be pretty macho," she adds. "One guy told me that because I do not have the male genes, I would not be able to run as fast as he could." A smile crosses her face. She says, "I would like to see him again. I want to pass him on a hill and ask him how his male genes are doing."

I ask her if a woman will one day beat the best man in a long foot race. Ann thinks it will happen. She says, "It is possible for a woman to win a 50- or 100-mile race. The longer the race, the more equal we are. It will not be me, though. I don't have what it takes, the mental strength mostly. But I can't wait until it happens. I can't wait!"

Ann is too modest. There is proof that she has plenty of mental strength. Think about this story she tells: "My boyfriend, Carl, and I were running in the Berkeley Hills. It was raining and I was hating it. I was just whining and suddenly Carl called me a wimp. A wimp! The Big W! I could not believe it. Right then I decided I was going to work to be a better hill climber than he was."

And that's what she did.

Ann is best-known for winning the foot race called the Western States 100. It is a 100-mile trail race through the Sierra mountain range. The whole race is up or down steep hills. It is over tree roots and rocks. The runners get thirsty and hungry. They sprain ankles. They get blisters on their feet. And they get sick from the altitude. Half the people who start the race don't finish.

Ann has won the race 2 times. She won it in 1990 in a time of 18 hours and 33 minutes. She beat all the women and 99.9% of the men. No woman has ever done that well against the men.

Ann has only a few sports heroes. There is a Greek man who she thinks is the greatest runner of all time. But the people she most admires are the final finishers in the Western States 100. After she finishes that race, she rests for many hours. Then she goes out to welcome in the last racers. She shakes her head and says, "I love to go out and watch the 29-30-hour finishers. They are great! I don't know how they do it. They see two sunrises! There is no way I could run that long!"

Most would say that she runs long enough. And in all the thousands of miles she has run, she has learned an important lesson. The race is really against herself. It is not about beating the clock, the course, or the other runners. It is about pleasing herself. It is about living up to her own standards. "My dad thinks I should do marathons so I could make some money. But then I would be against other people. In 100-milers I am racing against myself. You see, when you run a 100-mile race, finishing is always in doubt."

Steve McKinney on His Way Down!

Steve McKinney
Speed Freak

Steve McKinney was born to be a skier. He was raised among skiers—seven kids, seven skiers. But in Steve's family, it began at least 50 years before that. Steve's mother, Francis, has an old picture of Steve's grandmother going off a ski jump dressed in a skirt!

Steve's parents split up when he was five. His mom raised all seven kids. Steve said, "She was a strong woman. She believed in good health. She wanted us to be healthy in both mind and body. She was our teacher."

She was also her children's sports guide. They rode horses and skied. She started a ski school. She put her own kids on skis soon after they could walk. Steve recalls that his older sisters would ride a horse and tow him behind on his skis.

Steve grew up fast and hard. By the time he was 14, he was getting into trouble. He was a rebel. But he also had a great body. He was very strong. And he could ski like the wind.

After high school, he decided to become a ski racer. He set a goal and went for it. He tried out for the United States Ski Team. He made it. He was only 18 years old.

Steve was a great skier, but he did not like being on the team. He did not like taking orders. He thought it was too much like the Army. He said, "I couldn't figure it out. Why did I have to have a Marine haircut to race for the United States?"

He quit the team. Just before a World Cup race, he packed his backpack. He thumbed a ride to San Francisco. Then he caught a boat to Alaska. He was going to live alone in the woods. He would hunt and fish. He would take care of himself. He did not need help from others—or so he thought.

Steve recalls, "It rained for two straight weeks. It drove me nuts. I started to miss the spring skiing at Squaw Valley. I thought, 'What am I doing here?' When I got no answer, I went back home. I even took up rock climbing."

Steve was a good rock climber. He had big strong hands. And he had a good feel for the rock. He could focus his mind on the next move. But, like a lot of rock climbers, he had a fall. He fell 40 feet. That is like falling from the fourth floor of a house. He landed on a slab of rock and broke his back.

Some people would have quit sports after a broken back. Most people would have spent the rest of their lives on level ground. But Steve knew he would climb and ski again. He could always find something good in the bad things that happened to him. He could always see the bright side.

He was put in a body cast from his waist to his neck. He could not ski. That is what the doctors told him.

He decided to go to Italy. He had heard about a ski race where there were no turns. The skiers just went down the mountain as fast as they could. Speeds were twice what he was used to.

In his cast, he watched an Italian win the race. The winner's time was 114 miles per hour. Right then Steve decided that was what he wanted to do. He wanted to be the fastest skier in the world. He said, "When I first started skiing, I went for the fastest downhill courses. Then I went for the fastest parts of the fastest downhill courses. But even then I got tired of turns. Without speed I was bored."

No more would he be bored. He was now a speed skier. He was so excited that he even skied on that first trip to Italy. He skied in a body cast! "The cast taught me good form. It made me ski with my upper body stiff. I was forced to use only my legs. I learned to ski quietly, my body riding smooth and balanced," Steve said.

When he got out of his cast, he began to ski faster and faster. His 6-foot 2-inch, 190-pound body was made for speed. So he went back to Italy.

———————————

Steve stood near the top of the ski slope in Italy. He was waiting his turn to race down the mountain. He was wearing borrowed clothes and a borrowed helmet. He had been skiing his whole life. But he had never skied anything like this before. The race was straight down the mountain. There were no turns. From the top, it looked as steep as the side of a building. This was called speed skiing.

He would be the third racer to go. While he

waited, he took deep breaths. He also stretched his muscles. It helped calm him. Nearby, an Italian racer crossed himself and prayed. "Whatever works for you," thought Steve.

Yes, he had to think hard about his race against the clock. This was the fastest skiing in the world. Steve hoped to go more than 100 miles per hour. A mistake at that speed could cost him his life. He knew that more now than ever. He had to stay alert!

The next racer went down the hill. Now it was Steve's turn. He checked his skis for about the tenth time. They had to be right. After all, his life was riding on them. No matter what he might say later, this was scary. He was breathing fast and deep. So he used his mind to slow his breaths. Then he stepped into place.

He looked down the steep track. The flags that lined the course looked too close! The track looked too narrow! Could that be right? He stared for a minute. Yes, it was right. It was just his mind playing tricks. He snapped on his helmet and waited. His breathing was even now. He was in control.

The starter gave the word. Steve pushed off with his poles. He took four quick skating steps. The hill was white and very steep. It was like skiing off the end of the earth. Steve dropped into his tuck. After that, he started going really fast.

In his tuck, Steve's chest was on his knees. His arms were in front, breaking the air for his body. His head was low, but not too low. He kept his eyes up so he could see the track. He was flying down the mountain. His skis barely touched the snow.

He felt good. He felt in control. He lifted his butt a little. That helped push him forward and made him go faster. Of course, there was a risk. A head-first fall might kill him.

His speed rose above 100 miles per hour . . . 110 . . . 115 . . . To those standing near the track, Steve looked like a blur. He sounded like a missile. To Steve himself, all was quiet and still. Later he would call it "a touch of heaven."

He blew through a timing light like a bullet. He had reached 117 miles per hour. It was a new record.

In his skiing career, Steve set the speed record 5 times. He went almost 130 miles per hour on a pair of skis!

How fast is 130 miles per hour? Most of us have no idea. Compare it to these speeds:

The speed limit for cars in most places is 55 miles per hour.

The fastest speed of an Olympic downhill ski racer is 64 miles per hour.

A skydiver free falls about 120 miles per hour.

Steve loves how it feels to go fast. He has said, "Speed—I mean going fast, not the drug—is very healthy for me. It cleans my body and mind. It gives me a whole new look on life. It is like a cold bath."

But Steve is not just some crazy guy who gets his kicks going fast all the time. He can slow down, too. He has climbed Mt. Everest, the tallest mountain in the world. That kind of climbing is very slow. The climbers have to haul tons of gear up the mountain. It takes months for a group to get someone to the top of the world.

One time Steve climbed Mt. Everest for another reason. He wanted to hang glide off the mountain. He and his crew hauled up a bunch of 60-pound hang gliders. Those are kites that you strap yourself to so that you can fly like a bird.

Steve and his crew set the gliders up at about 26,000 feet above sea level. Nobody had ever soared off a mountain so high. Up there the air is very thin. Steve didn't know if there was enough air to support him and his glider. But he was willing to find out.

As it turned out, there was enough air. Steve and some others soared down into the valleys of Tibet. "It was the last and best adventure on Mt. Everest. The mountain had been climbed from every side. It had been skied. But before we got there, it had never been flown," he says.

So now Steve was a skier, a climber and a pilot. All three had to face bad falls. It must be scary. How does Steve get over the fear? Mostly, it seems, he just believes. He believes that he is going to be all right. He believes he is not going to fall. He believes in himself.

He did fall once at a high speed. He explained, "I do not wear gloves when I ski. It helps me feel my way. When I fell I did not think about that. I put my hands down in the snow to break my fall. But at 100 miles per hour, it was like putting them on a hot stove. I got a bad burn."

Does Steve ever worry about dying?

He laughed. "Fear is always trying to grab you. When you outsmart it, it sure feels good. I am not going to keep from doing things I should do because I fear death."

His friend and fellow racer, Tom Simons, has said, "I want to live, there is no doubt of that. But I have this way of thinking that it is O.K. to die. If I did not think that, I could not do what I do. Every racer knows his life is on the line."

"That is true," adds Steve. "We value our lives. I will take every step to protect my life—except for one. I will not stay home."

Steve McKinney was killed in 1990. A car crashed into the back of his parked VW Rabbit. The car was driven by a drunk driver.

Jericho Poppler Riding a Big One!

Jericho Poppler
Wave Rider

Jericho Poppler stood on the white sands of Hawaii's Sunset Beach. She was 15 years old. She watched the biggest waves she had ever seen break against the shore. They sounded like bombs. She could feel the rumble under her feet.

It was lovely there. The sand was as white as sugar. The waves were blue with white tips. The sky was the brightest blue she had ever seen.

Some would call the beach a paradise. But Jericho was not there as a tourist. She there to do a job. She was there to do what she does best. Jericho was there to ride waves because she was a pro surfer.

Sunset Beach had what survers called the "Big Waves." They were the biggest in the world. Only a dozen women in the world could ride those waves. Jericho was one of them. That is, she hoped she was one of them. At the moment, she had doubts.

She knew that she had to change her way of thinking. She had to believe that she could do it. No, she had to *know* that she could do it. If not, she could die out there.

It took her five minutes to paddle her board out past the biggest waves. That part of the sea was called the "safety zone." It was from there that she would start to surf back to shore.

As she paddled out, she looked over at some of the other women doing the same thing. She thought that they looked more sure of themselves than she did. Of course, most of them lived in Hawaii. They could surf the big waves every day. That had to help them. On the other hand, this was Jericho's first time.

Jericho thought of what one surfer said. "Waves are measured not in feet but in levels of fear." In other words, the bigger the wave, the greater the fear. Jericho had her share of fear. But she planned to make that fear work for her. Fear made her focus. Fear made her tough. That was just the way she was. She knew she was not going to quit. More than that, she knew she was going to try to win.

Just then a smooth, blue mountain of water lifted her way up high. Then, like a gentle giant, it dropped her into a deep valley of water. She thought, "Good golly, these waves are big!"

———————

Jericho grew up playing sports in California. She was a dancer by the time she was 5 years old. She was hitting home runs in softball by the time she was 9 years old.

Her father used to take her on two-week

hikes in the mountains. She says, "Dad wanted to make sure I could take care of myself. He would take only a little bit of food on our hikes. I had to find or catch food to survive. He did it to challenge me."

He taught her handball, tennis, and golf for her eye-hand skills. He taught her chess to make her think. But then she found a sport of her own.

It was a water sport, which made sense. Jericho grew up on the beach. Her bedroom overlooked the Pacific Ocean. All year long, she could watch swimmers and surfers from her room. She says, "I was always a beach gal. I got to see the ocean change every day. I fell in love with it."

Jericho became a strong swimmer. Many of her friends went on to win swimming races. But she did not love swimming as a sport. It was too boring. You had to swim hours and hours to be really good. She was just not willing to do it.

She wanted a more exciting sport. She decided she would try surfing. At that time in 1964, only males surfed. When Jericho showed up with a surf board, the guys made fun of her. She recalls, "The guys thought, 'Uhhh, a chick!' They did not like it at all. They told me girls should not surf. It hurt my feelings. I thought, 'I am going to beat you guys so bad, so bad.' "

Surfing is not an easy sport to learn. First, you have to stay on the board. It takes a lot of balance. But on her very first wave, Jericho rode the board all the way in to the beach. She did not fall off once. Did that make her feel great!

She didn't show up for dinner that night. Her brother had to go find her. It was dark and she was still surfing. "I was out in the ocean 5 straight hours. I was playing like a dolphin," she says.

Jericho fell in love with surfing. If she was not in school, you could find her at the beach catching waves. Her mother described a busy day in the life of her teen daughter. "She would wake up at 5 in the morning. She would surf until 7:30, then go off to school. After school, she was out surfing until dark. After she did her homework, it was off to bed. She was asleep quite early. She did not have too much fun," she says.

Jericho says, "It's all true, except for the last part. I had lots of fun! What could be more fun than surfing?"

Besides fun, surfing gave Jericho something that belonged all to her. Surfing made her feel good about herself. She says, "I loved the stuff my dad taught me. But surfing was all mine."

Surfing also gave Jericho an image. It was like playing a role in a movie. She knew just who she was. She was a "surfer girl." She liked that. She began dressing like a surfer. She listened to surfer music by the Beach Boys and Jan and Dean. And she began talking like a surfer. She used words like "dude" and "boss."

But Jericho did not just talk like a surfer. She acted like a surfer. Most of all, she acted just like one when she was riding the waves. "Riding a wave is like hitting a home run," she thought.

When Jericho was 14, she entered her first surfing contest. She didn't really want to enter. She was happy riding waves alone or with a few friends. She liked feeling free. She liked "playing" in the water. She didn't want to compete. But if a person is good, people think that person should compete. And so she did.

She did well in local contests. It made her want to do even better. Her mother and father urged her to keep going. She set a goal for herself. "I want to be U.S. Women's Surfing Champ," she said with a smile.

Before she could become champ, she had to

prove herself. She had to ride the Big Waves in Hawaii.

In Hawaii, Jericho kneeled on her board and waited for the right wave. They were all big, but some had better shape than others. One of the waves would be the perfect wave.

She was 5 foot 3 inches and 115 pounds. She had a hard stomach. She also had great back and leg muscles. She was strong. But she still looked tiny next to the huge waves. They looked like they could break her like a match stick.

But Jericho knew what she was doing. She was a strong swimmer. And she knew how to use the power of the waves to help herself. The biggest risk was from her surf board. If she fell, she could get hit in the head with her own board. If that happened, she might die.

It had happened to a woman surfer that Jericho knew. The woman had gone to Hawaii to ride the biggest waves in the world. She was out one day when a storm hit. The storm brought even bigger waves than usual. The woman tried to ride one of the waves into shore. She fell off. Her board hit her in the head. After that, she was like a flea in a blender. The waves tossed her here and there. The police found her body the next morning. It was 7 miles away.

Jericho didn't want to think about her friend. Instead she focused on the waves. They were 20 feet high from the front. But they were 40 feet high from the back. And that was the way Jericho was looking at them. "This is like looking over the edge of a 4-story building. And I have to take that first step," she thought.

It was not easy. Her heart was pounding like a drum. She was afraid, all right. But she refused to let the fear win. Besides, there was only one way to get in to shore. She had to ride her board.

She thought, "Once you take off on a wave, the fear is gone." Then she jumped onto her board. She rose to her feet. Now she was thinking only of what she had to do. She had to ride that wave.

She picked the biggest wave of the set. She glided along the peak of the wave. Then she free-fell down the face of the wave. For an instant, her feet were not touching her board.

Her feet again touched the board at the bottom of the wave. She cranked a hard right turn. She did that by shifting her body weight. Then she glided back up the face of the wave.

She flowed with the wave back to the bottom. She had the grace of a dancer. But her dance floor was the ocean. And it was moving all over the place.

Then the wave began to make a tube. Suddenly she was in the tube! Water flowed all around her. Surfers call that tube the "Green Room." It is the best place to be. Judges give extra points to surfers who find the Green Room.

Jericho flowed out of the tube. She was near the beach now. She kicked her board away from herself. With a big smile on her face, she threw her fist into the air. She thought it was the happiest she had ever been.

John Howard's Dad Watches Him Win

John Howard
Pedal Pusher

Since he was a kid growing up in Missouri, John Howard has wanted to go faster and farther on a bike than anybody. He got his first bike when he was in the first grade. But it was a clunker. It was a 3-gear Schwinn. It was not built for speed or distance.

When John and his brother were in high school, they started their own business. When the weather was good they did landscaping. When it was bad they cut and sold firewood. They put their profits into a pair of the new ten-speed touring bikes that had just hit the market.

John continued to play football, baseball,

and run track. But his love affair with the bike was for real. Soon he was riding his bike more and playing team sports less. When that happened, people started looking at him in a different way.

John says, "Springfield, Missouri, in the 1950's was very straight. In high school, riding my bike everywhere instead of driving a pickup truck got me branded a weirdo." He smiles. "I never cared too much. I like playing the crazy."

It was not just John's friends who thought he was weird. His track coach came down hard on him, too. John remembers it well. "Coach thought I was riding my bike too much. So he gave me a choice of biking or running the mile. I chose biking." Later when he quit football, his father almost had a heart attack.

After high school, John set his sights on bicycling in the 1968 Olympics in Mexico City. He began to train hard. He rode 400-500 miles a week. He was testing the limits of his endurance. "I made cycling a total commitment," he says.

In the summer of 1968, John left home. He traveled to Los Angeles for a pre-Olympic cycling race. He had to do well here if he wanted to make the Olympic team. He had to finish in the top four in one of two 100-mile road races.

In the first race, a young, unskilled John Howard finished way back in the pack. In the second race, a still young but no longer unskilled John came from behind to finish second. He was 20 years old. He was now on the Olympic team.

So began John's reign as America's number one cyclist. For the next ten years, he was the best in his sport in the United States. He has been in three Olympic Games, and he has won seven National Championships. He also did something that no other American has ever done. He won a gold medal in individual cycling at the Pan Am games.

But something still troubled him. Then one day it struck him. He was still on a "team." As a kid, he had said no to football and baseball because they were team sports. He had gone into cycling because he wanted to do it on his own. But being on the Olympic team meant he had to work with others. It also meant he had to be on a team again.

His coach noticed that he wasn't happy. He dumped him from the team. John's feelings were hurt. But he felt better when he remembered something his father had told him. "One day you outgrow everything."

Even though John did not want to be on a team, he still liked to compete.

He could not just settle down to a 9-to-5 job. He could not just forget about sports. So he decided to try a new sport, the Ironman Triathlon. It was really three sports in one. First, John had to swim 2.4 miles in the sea.

Then he had to bike 112 miles. After that, he had to run 26.2 miles on the hard pavement. It would take him more than 8 hours to do the Ironman.

"I just decided to do it. I didn't know anything about the sport. But I was sure I could win," he says.

He started working out harder than ever. Every week he rode his bike 400 miles and ran 70 miles. But the swim was his biggest worry. He says, "I put some time in the pool. But I didn't get a coach. So I had bad, bad form. I was not a good swimmer."

He still won the Ironman in 1981. That was amazing for someone who was a bad swimmer. When John started the bike part of the Ironman, he was in 750th place. After the bike part, he was in 1st place. He passed 749 people. He was some biker.

Next, he and some friends decided to have a bike race from Los Angeles to New York! They would race coast to coast, stopping only when they had to. It was about 3,000 miles from start to finish. They called it the Race Across America (RAAM).

It took John 10 days 11 hours. He finished in second place. He thought he should have been first. It still bothers him. "My crew was too soft on me. They let me have about three hours sleep a night. It was too much," he says.

Next he decided to go for the 24-hour cycling record. He dared world-class cyclists to meet him in New York's Central Park. "None of them showed up. They knew what would happen. I was in great shape," he says.

He proved that by riding 475 miles. It was a new 24-hour record. He has since done 519 miles in 24 hours.

Next John wanted to ride a bike faster than anyone had ever done it. He wanted to set the land speed record. So off he went to Utah.

John Howard jammed his big strong hands into his leather gloves. He looked out at the hot salt beds. It was July and hotter than 100 degrees. Wearing his leather clothes, he was hot and tired of waiting. He had been waiting for two days. First they were ready, then they were not. Now what was wrong? If it wasn't the bike, it was the car, or the wind, or the salt.

John was at the Bonneville Salt Flats in Utah to break the bicycling speed record. Some wondered why he went in the summer. It was so darn hot! But summer was also the only time he could count on the salt's being right. And when you went over 100 miles per hour on a bike, you wanted things to be right.

It was the waiting that bothered him. For every four-minute ride, there was a wait of three or more hours. It had to be done, of course. He knew that. His life was on the line. They had to keep the bicycle and the car clean of salt. Still, he wished they could get on with it.

He took off his big black gloves and took a drink from his water bottle. It was hard to drink enough water. Somebody figured that John sweated away four to five pounds on every ride.

At last, the Green Light! John's partner, race car driver Rick Vesco, started the car. The car, nicknamed Streamliner, was a 560-horsepower machine. Its top speed was more than 800 miles per hour. The rear of the car swooped up and out to look like a box. There, out of the wind, John would pedal his bike. That pocket of thin air behind the race car was called the "slipstream." Without a slipstream, the bicycling speed record was only 62 miles per hour.

John's bike was odd. It was small. But it cost $10,000. It had two chains and four sprockets. That gave him very low gears. Next

48

to the car, the bike looked tiny. John, a slim 6 feet 2 inches, looked huge sitting on it. He looked like an adult on a child's bike.

The roar of the car was loud and deep. It sounded like a group of hungry lions. An aide hooked a three-foot tow cable from the car to the bike. John, bathed in sweat, dropped his helmet visor. He then flicked a switch on his handlebars that gave him radio contact with Vesco in the car.

"Ready, Rick?"

"Ready, John. How about you?"

John smiled, nodded, and said, "Getting close. Got a feeling."

Then he waved and they began to move. Vesco went faster and faster, pulling John behind him. John could have pedaled from 0 to 60 under his own power. But the effort would have left him wasted for the high-speed struggle ahead.

John hit 60 miles per hour. He pushed the

lever to release the tow chain. Now he was on his own. And now he had to pedal very fast.

He also had to keep the front wheel of his bike within 10 inches of the car. He needed perfect touch. He would crash into the car if he went too fast. He would fall from the slipstream if he went too slow. Strong winds would probably knock him off his bike if that happened. And if he fell off his bike, he could die.

70 . . . 80 . . . 90 . . . He pedaled harder and faster. He tried to keep an even distance behind the car. His attention was total. Nothing else mattered.

100 . . . 110 . . . 120 . . . He was in the slipstream, but it was far from calm there. People thought it was a vacuum, but powerful winds still tried to push him off his bike. Staying on Vesco's tail was a terrible strain on his arms and shoulders. He had to be ready to adjust at once if Vesco veered a few inches.

130 . . . 140 . . . The record is ours, he thought. But suddenly he felt something strange! It seemed like the rear wheel was sinking into the sand. And the front one wanted to fly into the air. He dropped a few feet behind the race car and the wind hit him like a fist. Only his great upper-body strength kept him on the bike.

Vesco and his crew found him sitting on the sand, a wide smile on his face. "That's great!" Vesco said, laughing. "You just set a world record. You had the fastest flat tire on a bike. I had you doing 150!"

After that, most people would have given up speed cycling for a slower sport, but not John Howard. He figured he had just survived the worst thing that could happen. The flat tire was nothing but a confidence booster for John.

Two tries later, John set a new world speed record. He went 152 miles per hour. It was the exact figure he had seen in his dreams.

He later said, "I would have tried another run. But by then I'd had a couple of glasses of champagne. I didn't want to be unsafe."

These days, John travels around the country giving pep talks. He tells others how to succeed in sports. He hopes what he says will help them succeed in life.

He says he has tried to help others break his land speed record. But so far no one has come close. "Of course I want someone to break it. Where is the drama in breaking your own record? I want someone else to break it. Then I'll come back and put it away for good. I think 200 miles per hour is possible," he says.

That's just the way John talks. He is direct, honest, forceful, and confident. He has a lean, firm jaw and cool blue eyes that seem to look right through you. He seems to be saying, "This is the way it is. Go talk to someone else if you don't like it."

John Howard is brave but not fearless. His biggest fear is that he will not go fast enough or far enough. His desire to break a record is stronger than his fear of getting hurt.

He also just loves bicycling. Listen to what he says about the sport. "There is something about covering a lot of ground under your own power. It has to do with the blue sky, the fresh air, the gears working just right. It gives you a great feeling. And once you have found it, nothing else will do."

That's the way a world-class pedal pusher talks.

Jon Lugbill—All Wet But a Winner!

Jon Lugbill
River Rat

The alarm clock went off at 6:00 a.m. just as it did every morning. Jon Lugbill rolled his tired body out of bed. It was hard to believe that in fifteen minutes he would be paddling his covered canoe on the icy Potomac River.

He dressed quickly and went outside. It was April. There was frost on the ground and a nip in the air. Jon wore shorts, no socks. Soon he would be working too hard to be cold.

He lifted his canoe onto his shoulder. He began carrying it the half-mile down to the river. It was not light yet. He passed the houses of many of his school mates. They were still asleep. That made sense. None of them was trying to become the best white-water paddler in the world.

Jon reached the river. There was no one else there. He set his canoe down at the edge of the water. A bird called from the bushes. The water made a rushing sound. Except for that, it was quiet.

He enjoyed nature for a few seconds. Then he climbed into his canoe. It had a spray skirt over it that kept the water out of the boat. All that showed was the top half of Jon's body. Under the skirt, Jon kneeled. His legs and feet scraped on the boat bottom.

He took his paddle in his hands. It had a blade at only one end. (Kayak paddles have blades at both ends.) He thrust the paddle into the river and pushed off. This part of the river was not moving real fast. It was his practice area.

He and others had hung up "gates." A gate was two poles hanging near each other. They looked like baseball bats painted red and green. They dangled in pairs over the river. Every few feet there were two more. Jon tried to put his boat between two poles. Then he tried to go between the next two. He did it as fast as he could. It took a big effort. His heart was pounding.

Jon went through the gates going both upstream and downstream. He did it from all angles. Then he did it over again. He stayed in the boat so long his feet began to bleed.

Then he went off to school.

The Lugbill family's first boat race took place when Jon was ten years old. His father entered an "Anything That Floats" race. So Mr. Lugbill and his three sons tied 30 inner tubes together. They called it a raft. But then Jon and Ron, the two youngest sons, were not allowed to race. They were too young. So Dad and his oldest son started the race. They finished dead last.

Jon entered his first canoe race when he was 12 years old. He will never forget it. "The water was 35 degrees. I fell out of the boat twice. I finished last. It was bad," he says.

But he stayed with it. He began paddling a two-man canoe with his brother Ron. They entered races. They didn't win, but they got to practice their strokes.

When Jon was still a young kid, he saw a racer die in the water. He says, "The guy lost his boat. He swam, then he tried to walk out of the river. He got caught under a rock. The current broke both of his legs and he drowned."

Some kids would have quit right then. But not the Lugbills. They kept paddling. They even asked their parents to let them go to a training camp in Colorado. Their mom and dad were always willing to help. They said yes. They even paid for the camp.

Jon recalls, "We learned a lot at that school. They taught us how to take care of ourselves in fast, tough water. It made us bold."

One big lesson they learned was, "Do not swim." Even if they tipped over, they should stay in the boat. Jon says, "You are supposed to roll the boat over. Any time you swim in white water, you are out of control. Now I never leave the boat."

Jon and Ron kept learning. And they kept getting better. While their school friends were playing ball games, they were working on their paddle strokes. Jon says, "We kept at it because it was fun. At first, we were not trying to get really good. We were just trying to have fun."

By the time Jon was in the 9th grade, he had reached his adult size. He was 5 feet 9 inches and 175 pounds. He had broad shoulders and big arm muscles. His legs were strong, too, but smaller. In his sport, he used his arms a lot more than his legs.

When Jon was 14, the East Coast had a real warm winter. The water in the lakes and rivers did not freeze. So the boys could paddle all year long. They hung 3 pairs of poles above the pond near their house. They worked out 5 days a week. They practiced paddling the canoe through the gates. They learned to guide the paddle through the water at just the right angles.

Jon hated losing. But he also hated doing a move wrong. He hated being sloppy. He wanted to practice over and over until he did it right. With that much practice, Jon and Ron began to see results. They got much better.

Then something amazing happened. Jon, who was 14 years old, and Ron, 16, qualified for the White Water World Championships. "We couldn't believe we had made the United States Team. We were in complete shock," says

Jon with a laugh.

At the World Championships in Yugoslavia, the Lugbill teenagers did not do well. They finished 22nd out of 26 boats. That was no surprise. No United States boats had ever done well at the World Championships. But that was no excuse. Jon was not happy.

Jon talked to the other athletes. He found out that they didn't like their sport very much. They liked being on their country's team, but they did not like to practice. They didn't have fun. To Jon, that didn't make sense. "If you don't love it, why do it?" he likes to say.

The next World Championships were in two years. Jon and Ron were sure they would be better by then. "We knew if we trained right, we'd blow those guys away," Jon says.

In order to train right, they needed a coach.

Then one day, when Jon was in high school, a man moved in down the street from the Lugbills. His name was Bill Endicott. He said he was a paddling coach. He was tall and wore glasses. He had rowed in college. Someone in his family had died and left him a lot of money. Now he could do whatever he wanted in his life. He knew right away what that was. He wanted to coach the best white-water paddlers.

And that is what he did.

Good coaches can bring out the best in athletes. Bill brought out the very best in Jon. He also brought out the best in other kids in the neighborhood. But Jon could go the fastest.

Jon moved on to the one-man canoe. Bill taught him that the sport was more than just forcing your way through the water. He taught him that it took more than brute strength. Paddling in white rapids sometimes took a soft touch. It took style.

So now Jon had more than strength. He also had a feel for the water and great technique. He won the World Championship the next year. In fact, he has gone on to win 6 world championships. He is the best white water canoe racer the world has ever seen.

Jon has been the best in his sport for more than 10 years. But being the best has brought him no fame and no fortune. Most people still have not heard of him. "I was on the back of two million Wheaties boxes. But that only lasted a month," he says.

It does not bother him that other athletes are more famous than he is. He just wishes people would get his sport right. He hates it when they say to him, "Are you still rafting?"

What has made Jon Lugbill so good? What has made him number one?

His coach thinks there are three main skills needed to be a great white water paddler. He says, "First, you need great upper-body strength. Second, you have to be able to 'read' the water currents and know where to put the paddle. Third, you need mental toughness. Jon has an athlete's mind. He does not panic. He can change his style to do new things in the water."

Jon has his own ideas. He thinks he knows why he is the best in the sport. He says, "It's simple. Paddling has always been fun for me. And that makes me willing to work harder."